Nature's Clean-Up Crew

The Burying Beetles

Close-up of a burying beetle

Nature's Clean-Up Crew

The Burying Beetles

Lorus J. Milne
and
Margery Milne

With photographs by the authors

Dodd, Mead & Company
New York

The pen-and-ink illustrations on pages 13, 18, 30–31, and 35 are by Tom Prentiss, reprinted with his permission and that of *Scientific American* from our article, "The Social Behavior of Burying Beetles," in the August, 1976, issue.

Library of Congress Cataloging in Publication Data

Milne, Lorus Johnson, date
Nature's clean-up crew.

Includes index.
Summary: Describes the physical characteristics,
reproductive life cycle, and behavior patterns of the
burying beetle, which functions as nature's clean-up
crew.
1. Burying beetles—Juvenile literature. [1. Burying
beetles. 2. Beetles] I. Milne, Margery Joan Greene,
date. II. Title.
QL596.S5M63   595.76′42   81–15127
ISBN 0–396–08038–3   AACR2

*For the Arthur Johnson Stephens family in Irondale,
Ontario, where we first discovered and observed
burying beetles, and to Bill Eastman, who
encouraged us to tell their story.*

Contents

Foreword

All living things are special. Each particular kind of creature stands out in some way. The distinctive feature about burying beetles, which fascinates everyone who observes them closely, is the amazing care they take for their young. This care shows a very advanced form, in a group of insects where such care is uncommon. Their antics and behavior deserve an award.

These insects are also called sexton beetles; scientists know them as *Nicrophorus*. Every creature has a two-word scientific name, which is used internationally. The first word is the genus which, for a burying beetle anywhere, is *Nicrophorus*. The second word is the species, indicating the particular kind of *Nicrophorus*. A common burying beetle found from Hudson Bay to Florida and from Indiana to the Atlantic coast is *Nicrophorus orbicollis*.

Some of the smaller burying beetles fly about by day

in most parts of the country, or they amble over the ground in search of food. Most burying beetles become active in darkness. Occasionally one flies to a lighted window and settles on the screen, without buzzing its wings as though to draw attention, as a May beetle does. Seen from indoors through the screen, the black under-surface of the beetle blends with the night.

Although burying beetles are a minority among the vast array of different insects, they become favorites to observe and admire. Each is handsome in the orange and black markings on its back, and strong and industrious. Its inherited behavior reveals patterns that enable the insect to cope with a wide variety of unusual situations. Its actions often come close to those that humankind terms "intelligent."

I.

Where Do All the Mice and Sparrows Go?

Every meadow is home to thousands of meadow mice and to a great many small birds too. The woodlands teem with different mice and sparrows. Yet rarely do we find a mouse or a sparrow that has reached the end of its brief life. Or, if we notice a dead bird that has flown into a picture window, or a mole that a cat has caught, only to discard the body, the remains often vanish overnight. Where do they go? Decay cannot work so fast. Bears and wild pigs are too few to attend to so much cleanup.

The disappearance is like magic. It begins soon after a bird tumbles lifeless from its perch in the forest onto the dark ground, or a mouse dies the same night among the leaf litter under the trees, or an old snake comes to final rest in the pasture, or a fish is tossed by storm waves high on the beach.

To the scientist, the "natural" death of an animal is interesting mainly as the first step in returning to the soil the raw materials of which the living body was composed. Bacteria and fungi start work at once, slowly and inconspicuously. Insects and other animals help at a faster pace, causing the reconversion of the dead body into new life. All of these orderly activities are necessary in keeping the raw materials in circulation.

Among the most spectacular ways in which this is accomplished is through the activity of certain insects. Each is a sturdy black beetle about an inch long, usually banded with bright orange across its back.

The beetle picks up the faint odor of decay in the air, and flies toward the body, directing its flight by sensitive feelers. Arriving like a little helicopter, the insect circles and lands, seldom more than thirty-six inches from its target. Through the undergrowth the beetle pushes its way. It pays no attention if some person is there watching, waiting for the magic to begin. Knowing what to expect is helpful. "What we see is mostly what we look for," as Sir John Lubbock noted a century ago. Recently a young friend proved this, when he burst into the house, breathless with excitement. "Come quick! A beetle is carrying away a dead mouse."

We followed our friend out the door to a place where the grass had been worn away, making a path with bare ground. There was the mouse on its back, its pale underside contrasting with the ground. Yet the mouse was moving, little by little. Whatever caused the movement was hidden

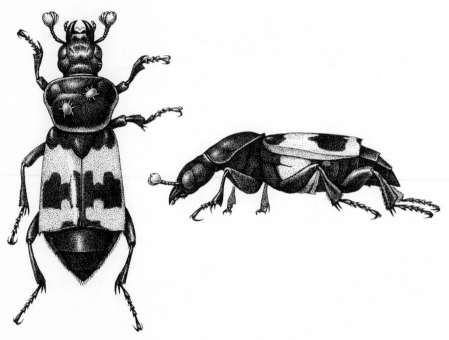

Burying beetle shown from above and side. Note the markings.

underneath, lifting and shifting one small portion of the body at a time, the twitchy movement finally reaching the rear end of the mouse. Out slid a black beetle. Quickly the insect righted itself, revealing the two bright orange bands across its shiny wing covers. The sturdy beetle ran around the mouse to the head, crawled under, turning upside down as it did so.

With its back against the ground, the beetle used its strong legs like levers to lift the head of the mouse and shift it forward slightly. Gradually the beetle skidded against the supporting earth, always farther toward the rear of the mouse. Continually it lifted and moved the

A burying beetle investigating body of dead white mouse

body, invariably in the same direction. The mouse progressed fully half an inch before the beetle emerged once more near the tail, and ran forward as though ready to repeat its action.

"Four minutes," said somebody. "I timed it. That would be fifteen passes under the mouse each hour. Moving half an inch each time, the body would travel nearly eight inches in the hour, or twelve inches in an hour-and-a-half. How far would that get before dawn tomorrow?"

This time the beetle did not stay with its task. It ran right past the head of the mouse. The agile insect kept on over the hard bare ground, into some straggly grass.

14

The green blades were serious obstacles. They made the beetle struggle, and slowed its advance. Yet the insect kept going until it reached an old abandoned flower bed with only a few weeds. Between the weeds the beetle shoved its flat head into the soil. With all six legs pushing vigorously, the insect scrambled along just beneath the surface. It loosened the earth and pushed it upward, without dislodging much. This new action continued for several minutes. Then the beetle emerged into the open and used its feet to tidy itself. It cleaned away every particle of soil sticking to its body. Immediately it hurried back through the grass tangle to the mouse. Without hesitation, the insect turned upside down beneath the head and started once more to shift the mouse over itself, bit by bit.

Within two hours, the beetle moved its mouse to the end of the bare soil and began to work it through the straggly grass. Every green blade provided some resistance. The beetle bent each grass blade, either aside or under the body of the mouse, and kept on moving it. Progress slowed to a quarter inch in four minutes. Yet always the movement was in the same direction. At intervals the beetle took time out, leaving the mouse to loosen more soil in the flower bed.

On one of these occasions when the dead mouse was unattended, another insect came buzzing out of the darkness. The flier circled above the mouse and dropped to the ground. At once the insect folded its wings and began to force its way between the grass blades toward the mouse. The newcomer was another beetle like the first,

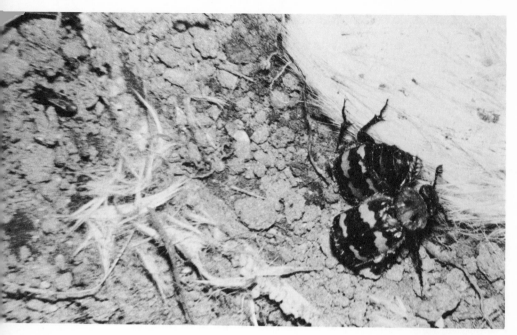

Encounter between two beetles exploring body of white mouse

perhaps a trifle smaller. It ran up to the body of the mouse, touched it along one side with sensitive feelers, and turned upside down to crawl through underneath. By these maneuvers the beetle sensed that the body was small enough to manage, and free to move. Two minutes later, the newcomer was lifting and shifting the body. Even before the two beetles met, they seemed to be cooperating partners. They both moved the mouse in the same direction.

The first beetle returned and discovered its companion. Suddenly we heard faint scratchy sounds, as though the two were communicating with one another in a secret code. The beetles separated. Both began to move the mouse

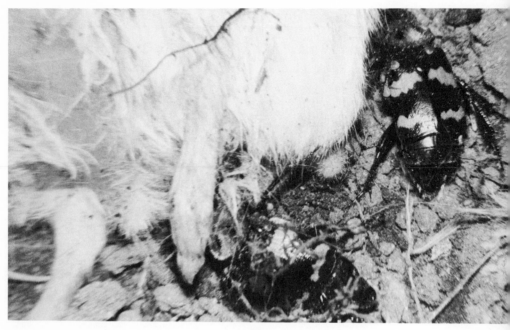

Two beetles exploring under edge of body of dead white mouse

along. It shifted faster with two workers. We felt sure they were willing partners.

By midnight, the beetles and their mouse reached the flower bed where the one insect had already loosened several square inches of surface soil. Soon they had the mouse over that exact area, and stopped shifting it. Instead, both beetles crawled under the mouse and began shoving out earth to all sides. They worked steadily, like six-legged bulldozers. The body of the mouse sagged into the shallow grave as the beetles dug. Their trench got deeper, and the mouse went down into it.

One ear of the mouse caught on the rim of the trench.

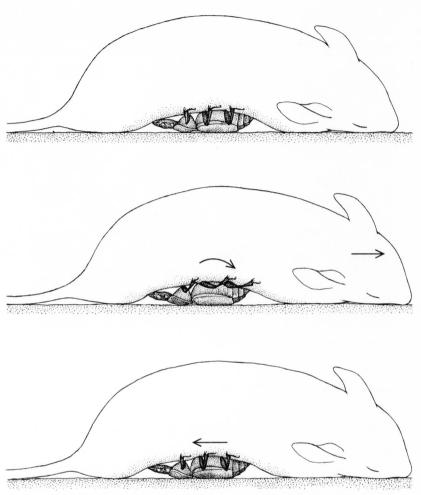

Transport of carcass by burying beetle lying on its back. It uses its legs like levers to shift the body forward.

Surprisingly, it was stiff enough to hinder movement. Surely the insects would chew off the ear as worthless, or dig a special groove for its descent. For a while the beetles did not identify this obstacle to their progress. They solved

18

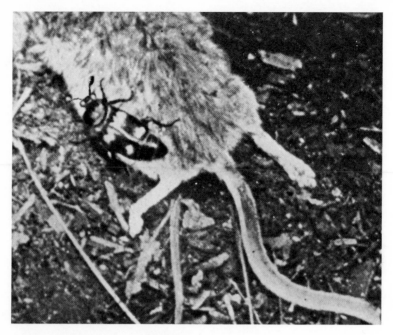

Beetle running over back of dead gray mouse

their difficulty by rotating the body of the mouse. They simply turned the head until the ear was downward, out of the way. Later the tail of the mouse caught on the end of the trench. The insects pushed the tail until it was U-shaped. No longer did it hinder the downward movement.

In just three hours the mouse vanished. It sank out of sight. The loose earth that had been pushed out around it on all sides fell on top of the dead body and concealed it. For a while this loose earth heaved every few minutes, showing that a beetle was crawling over the mouse below. Even this indication of activity ceased, as though the mouse had been taken deeper. It could be that the beetles pressed against their ceiling so often that it became firm, unyielding. Now the body of the mouse was in a burial chamber for sure. No one could guess it was there. The clean-up crew had their body where they wanted it before daylight. It was time for them to start a family.

2.

Beetle Magic

The feelers or antennae of a burying beetle are much more sensitive than a human nose. They alert the insect to the faintest odor of decay. This fragrance is absolutely irresistible to the beetle. The scent may come from a small bird or mammal that has been killed. It may have tried to cross the road just as an automobile was passing. Often the little body is flipped to bare ground. In midsummer the slight odor brings a burying beetle in less than half an hour.

Finding a dead mouse, a chipmunk, or a sparrow on soft soil is probably a rare event. The beetles must be ready to transport their prize to a suitable place. They can manage a dead sparrow just as easily as a dead mouse. A dead robin, bluejay, or skunk seems harder. A dead groundhog or a house cat is too big. A snake is a challenge for a cooperating group. Each small body is a manageable prize, to be hidden underground as quickly as possible. Only where the soil is hard must the body be shifted to a better location. This may require one beetle to move a mouse many times its own length and weight, as much as fifteen feet in a few hours.

The hard-working beetles seldom seem to relax. Any stick or stone in their way requires a detour. Each beetle shows itself extremely versatile in reacting to every challenge.

Frequently an overarching plant stem catches on a small body that the beetles are moving. First, the insects place themselves with their backs against the stem, legs in the fur. They strive to force some progress. If the stem will not stretch enough, one beetle gets busy chewing on the plant strand and continues until it gives way.

The actions of the busy beetles can be followed readily until they get their mouse or sparrow underground. The details were described first by a patient schoolteacher, Jean Henri Fabre, from his studies in southern France during the late 1800s. Repeatedly he set out bait: a dead frog, a lizard, a goldfish, a mutton cutlet, a strip of beefsteak, a mole begged from the gardener, all "in the right stage of maturity." On the many occasions when burying beetles arrived, they and the bait disappeared below the soil. This proved to Fabre that these insects have "no exclusive preferences." He came to admire the beetles, "elegantly attired" in black, with a "double, scalloped scarf of vermillion" across their shining wing covers.

For many years, scientists doubted the accuracy of

Beetle running along the ground close to body of gray mouse.
Note plant stem and leaf across body.

Fabre's stories, particularly because they were told in a peasant's simple way. Not until the 1930s did anyone repeat or improve upon Fabre's studies, or confirm the marvelous behavior shown by these insects underground. Yet burying beetles achieve their purposes in the same general way everywhere. They modify their tactics according to the situation. As Fabre noted, "To saw, to break, to disentangle, to lift, to shake, to displace: these are so many means which are indispensable to the grave-digger

Beetle bulldozing into soil to loosen it as a burial site

One beetle stretching leaf stalk of clover which limited free trans-
port of dead gray mouse; a second beetle at mouse's head end; a
fly ready to compete for use of carcass.

in a predicament. Deprived of these resources, reduced to uniformity of procedure, the insect would be incapable of pursuing its calling."

By working so hard all night, the beetles have a chance to avoid competitors for their prize. After the sun rises and warms the world, insects of other kinds go hunting for food. Ants and hornets would like to nip out pieces of

A burying beetle. Note its strong legs.

meat and carry them home. Flies come to lay masses of eggs, which soon hatch to hungry, legless maggots. Other flies hold their eggs until they hatch, and drop lively maggots on the dead body. Maggots quickly destroy the food supply needed by the larvae of the burying beetles.

This explains why the beetles always seem in such a hurry to inter each prize. Getting the body to soft ground and concealing it below the surface is too important to spend time on anything else first. Courtship and mating can wait. Almost any member of the opposite sex and same species will be acceptable, first as a helper, later as the parent of a family of young.

Although the competition by ants and flies is so much more severe by day, burying beetles of a few kinds try to meet it by being especially active then. Mostly these are smaller, barely three-quarters of an inch long. They usually resemble small bumblebees as they fly along. Dull golden hair covers black areas of the body above and along the sides below. If disturbed, a burying beetle of this type turns upside down, concealing its distinctive orange crossbands. It buzzes loudly, as though imitating a bumblebee that has been awakened early on a cool morning. Any creature that fears the stinger of a bumblebee is likely to avoid the beetle and take no chances. Usually the beetle stays quiet and motionless a while before trying again to go rushing about on its business. With luck it may get a small body underground before the competition arrives.

A buried mouse or sparrow is much less likely to be detected by ants, hornets, or flies. Somehow the earth itself absorbs most of the odors of decay and hides the prize from creatures that move about in air. The method that burying beetles inherit and follow so regularly really succeeds. Magically, it promotes nature's own great recycling, while providing for more burying beetles.

3.

Patient Parents— Undercover Activities

A Polish student at the Zoological Institute in Frankfurt-am-Main (West Germany) found a way to watch burying beetles in the darkness of their underground chamber. Erna Pukowski induced the insects to bury a dead mouse between two vertical panes of glass she had positioned less than an inch apart, with earth between them and on both sides. Although such a tight squeeze, the beetles managed. Later, Pukowski opened the earth on one side, exposing a glass pane. She removed it and saw into the beetles' secret lives. Her photographs and her report, which were published in 1933, earned her a doctor's degree.

Pukowski discovered that the mother beetle digs a short vertical tunnel directly above the body, into the soil covering the burial chamber. In the side walls of this extension, the beetle lays about fifteen eggs and leaves them to hatch. Meanwhile the father continues to remove all hair or feathers from the dead body. He stows them in a corner, out of the way. The two beetles work to shove their prize into an almost spherical form. Somehow they embalm it so that it will decay only slowly. Since beetles of this kind were in existence millions of years ago, we can assume that they were embalming small bodies long before the ancient Egyptians began embalming people, cats, and other animals as mummies.

Both parents feed from the top of their buried food supply, and eat out a shallow depression in the top. This becomes a saucer into which the beetles bring forth partly digested nourishment, as a special pabulum for their young. It accumulates in the depression, filling a tiny pool with fluid food.

When the eggs hatch, the parents make scratchy sounds by rubbing rough places on their wing covers against ridges on their bodies. The hatchlings hear the sound and crawl to their parents. If this scratchy noise is recorded and played back through a loudspeaker, the hatchlings will crawl toward it instead. Pukowski was able to see the young beetles, now called larvae, raise their heads like little birds and tap against the mouthparts of the parents. Promptly an adult brings forth a drop of food, much as a parent bird might. Or it picks up a little from the liquid pool and transfers it to the young larva.

The young grow quickly on such an abundant supply of rich nourishment. In a few weeks, each youngster

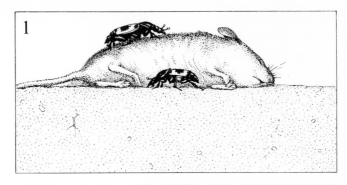

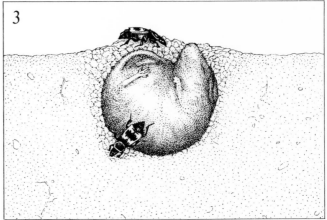

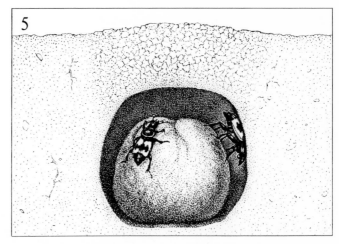

Sequence showing burial of mouse by two beetles.

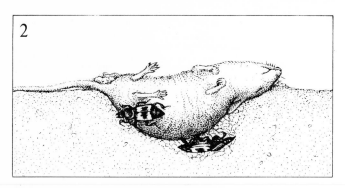

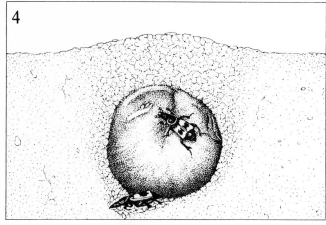

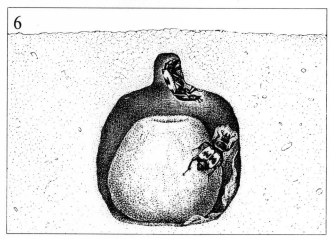

Eggs are laid in chamber above pool of liquid food.

reaches full size. Automatically it ceases to feed, and is ready to change form. In the total darkness of the chamber, the parent beetles sense that their young have reached this stage. Generally the parents dig a horizontal passageway to one side from the burial chamber, and lead their young into it. Each youngster takes up a position of its own along the side of the passageway and turns on its back. Its skin splits and shrivels up, revealing the doll-like pupa inside. This is a fasting stage. The parent beetles seem to take the change as a signal that they can do no more for their young. Each parent digs its way up through the soil to the outside world and flies away. Perhaps it will find another dead mouse or sparrow somewhere, meet a new mate, and begin another family.

If there were any light in the passageway, one could see grooves marking the surface of each pupa. They show a complex pattern, revealing which parts of the pupa will develop as the head, the antennae and jaws, the thorax, the wing covers and legs, and the abdomen of the adult insect. This development requires weeks, or months if the soil is cold because winter is at hand. But gradually the inner parts of the former larva are converted. They transform into those that will serve the mature insect.

Slowly the color of the pupa darkens, from pale ivory-yellow like that of the larva, to brownish red, to reddish brown, finally to black. The pupa begins to wiggle its legs, waving them in the air of the passageway. It gets ready to fend for itself, to be as successful as an adult as its own parents were. These transformations correspond to the

Beetle on ball-shaped remains of mouse in burial chamber, close to a single larva

change of a caterpillar to a chrysalis (a pupa) and then to a winged butterfly.

The greatest magic of all is that the inexperienced beetle needs no leader or instructions. It has only to roll over onto its legs and make its way upward through the soil from its pupal site into its future world. Its inheritance

Four larvae clinging to remains of mouse in burial chamber

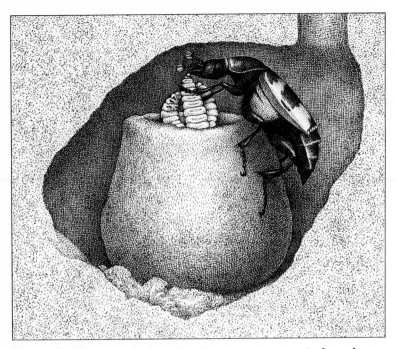

Parent beetle regurgitating liquid food for one of three larvae atop ball-shaped remains of mouse in chamber

will guide it for correct behavior as it walks or runs about nimbly. The beetle aims its sensitive antennae forward, their clublike tips checking the breeze for important odors. When ready, the beetle spreads its wing covers to the sides and forward. It extends its thin second pair of wings—its flying wings—from beneath. It vibrates these wings and begins flying. Now the insect's legs are folded neatly, held close to the underside of its body almost like the under-carriage of an airplane. Held in this position, they reduce to a minimum the amount of energy the insect must expend to continue flying. The beetle can concentrate on detecting

Close-up of two larvae beside foot of white mouse remains in burial chamber

the faint odor of decay or the delicate lure of another beetle—one that has already found a prize and needs help in burying it.

Scientists are amazed that the sexes of burying beetles are so alike in their behavior and importance. The female, of course, is the only one able to lay eggs. But the male is as capable and active as she is in finding a suitable dead body, in transporting or burying it, in embalming and caring for the food supply, in preparing the liquid food for the young, in summoning and feeding them, and in digging the side passageway in which the young will pupate when fully grown. He participates fully in all of these parental chores, not merely in fertilizing the eggs that his mate will lay. He is a model parent, not a temporary contributor, as is true of almost every other kind of insect and of many other animals as well. This cooperation between the sexes proves beneficial and continues as a special way of life. Today burying beetles adhere to this tradition on every continent except Australia, and Africa south of the great deserts, even on some islands in the East Indies and South Pacific. None of their near relatives shows any comparable behavior. None is so widely distributed over the earth.

Everywhere the food supply that parent burying beetles provide for their family of young seems more than generous. Rarely do the attending adults and the hungry larvae in the burial chamber use more than a third of the meat that is available, so compactly pushed into the shape of a ball with a depression in the top. The rest of the food is left untouched. Gradually it decomposes, adding to the soil various compounds of nitrogen and phosphorus. These hold great importance for the roots of plants. They are fertilizer, contributions to the welfare of vegetation by courtesy of insects. They are materials that the mouse or sparrow got while it was still alive, by eating fruits and seeds produced by plants. Now the materials are returning to the earth for another cycle through plants to animals.

4.

Opportunities for Observation

The amazing antics of burying beetles can be followed in many a vacant lot or home garden, as well as in the country. "Road kills," whether small mammals, a bird, or even a reptile such as a garter snake, serve well as bait. The snake will attract burying beetles even if it is placed in an empty wrapper from a loaf of bread, and tied to a tree limb several feet above the ground. The insects soon cut holes through the wrapper, and try to find a way to get the snake out, down to soft earth.

A snake already on the ground may be too heavy for the beetles to move elsewhere. On loose soil they may sink it where it lies. Yet rarely do two beetles attempt the whole job. Instead, they concentrate their efforts on either the front half of the snake or the back half. Wait a while. A second pair of burying beetles may fly in and attend to

Two burying beetles and a fly investigating body of road-killed bluejay. The beetles have already pulled a few feathers loose, making the body more manageable.

the remainder. The two pairs cooperate, each pair working only in its own territory.

Often the beetles get the body of the snake concealed before doing anything with the head or the tail. These offer little food, and are the last to be buried. Or they are left exposed. Sometimes a sharp-eyed person notices the tail of a snake sticking out of the ground. With a trowel, the snake can be exposed from tail to head. Usually this reveals also two pairs of burying beetles that are still in attendance. After discovering them, it seems proper to

Two beetles and a fly investigate body of dead garter snake.

cover the snake and beetles as they were. The insects will have to work hard enough to restore their burial chambers and to tend their families of young when their eggs hatch. They should benefit from having labored so long in getting the body of the snake underground.

Getting bait that will attract burying beetles is often a challenge, the first step toward seeing these energetic insects in action. One scientist in New Jersey gets chicken necks from the butcher shop, and sets them out in likely places. Seldom does anyone care if a mousetrap or two is

40

Beetles exploring body of snake before attempting burial

baited and placed inconspicuously in a field, a house lot, or along the edge of a woodland.

Peanut butter is a good bait. It appeals to many mice and keeps well. But the trap needs attention day and night, since the intention is to see burying beetles coming soon after a mouse gets caught. Sitting close to the trap as a guardian has advantages. By day in a pasture, a sheep may discover an untended trap and lick off the bait. The big animal enjoys peanut butter, especially if it is slightly salty. The trap snaps, frightening the sheep for a moment but not hurting it. Yet the trap now needs reloading and resetting if it is to catch anything. At night, a wandering skunk may be attracted to any trap that has caught a mouse. Unless a person is nearby as a guardian, the skunk will eat the mouse and perhaps carry away the trap.

Fortunately, burying beetles pay no attention to a human guardian. They will come to work on a dead mouse or sparrow that has been set atop some earth in a metal or plastic pan, even above ground or on a table. The rim of the pan should be two inches or more higher than the earth in the container, so that the beetles will not be tempted to shift the body over the rim. Then they will bury their prize in the container and attend to their family in the burial chamber. A young naturalist transported such a beetle family in a pan of earth about 800 miles by automobile without disturbing the insects, and continued observing them at home because time had run out for studies in the field.

Some people try to see what is going on below ground by getting the beetles to bury a small body in a transparent glass bowl. The plan succeeds if the insects happen to make the glass one side of their burial chamber. No doubt this is why Erna Pukowski provided her two glass panes so close together that a mouse buried between them would be squeezed against both sides. She kept everything as dark as it would be underground until the last moment, when she let light in to see what the beetles were doing.

Experiments to test the versatility of the beetles are easiest before burial is achieved. A strong string, for

42

Beetle chewing on strong string tied to hind leg of dead mouse, which makes burial difficult

example, can be tied to the leg of a dead mouse, and used to tether the animal to a tree or a stake. Beetles will push the earth from beneath the body until it hangs suspended. They rotate it one way, then the other, above their cup-shaped depression. Not until the mouse hangs above the space made for its burial is a beetle likely to discover the string or do anything about it. Then the insect will start chewing on the cord, although cutting through it will require hours of hard work. Usually before dawn, the

Close-up of beetle chewing on string

mouse is safely buried, still with a short piece of string around its leg.

A stone or a brick leaned up on the body of a dead mouse is more of a challenge. Yet a pair of beetles will force themselves into the tightest place, their legs against the fur, their backs against the hard surface. Often the insects squeak or click audibly as they labor to shift the mouse even an eighth of an inch at a time. At intervals, they change position to work between the mouse and the soil. Always, however, they move their prize in the same direction—until it is free. It may take all night, but the beetles do not give up easily.

Sometimes the actions of burying beetles come close to

being unbelievable. If someone sets out a small mousetrap in a flower bed and anchors the wooden platform of the trap to the soft soil by drilling a hole through the wood, big enough to easily accommodate a large nail driven into the ground, a mouse may still get caught and the beetles find it. The steel spring of the trap will prevent them from moving the mouse off the platform. The insects may simply push out the soil under the whole trap, letting it sink into the earth, mouse and all. So long as the platform goes down almost horizontally, it may not bind on the nail. If it does, the beetles keep working and eventually get their prize buried. Then only the vertical nail may project from the soil, revealing where the mouse (and the trap) are concealed.

In regions where burying beetles are so numerous that several arrive while one or a pair is moving a dead mouse to soft soil, it is tempting to pick up the largest beetle gently and to imprison it in a box for an hour or two. Other, smaller beetles will then transport the body while the captive is away. When the imprisoned beetle is released an inch or two from the dead mouse, its usual reaction is to lie motionless for a few seconds as though dead. Then it scrambles to its feet and extends its antennae. Often the insect starts out straight toward the mouse, wherever it is, proving how well the sense of smell gives the beetle its direction. If no larger burying beetle is present, the individual that has just been freed is likely to take charge and repel the rest. It seems to recognize the mouse as its own and to proceed as though nothing had happened.

Smaller of two beetles with wings spread, ready to fly away after confrontation with larger beetle

Close-up of smaller beetle with wings spread, ready to fly

A similar behavior may be shown if, while a burying beetle has temporarily gone from its prize to work in the soil at the burial site, the body of the dead mouse is moved a few inches to one side. The returning beetle seldom travels beyond where it last left the body. It tests the air, and usually goes straight to the mouse in its new location. A brief inspection, made by passing underneath from side to side several times, is customary before the next efforts at shifting the body toward the burial site.

If an extra mouse is available, it can be substituted for the one a burying beetle has been transporting. The change is noticed promptly. The insect generally begins hunting for its former trophy. If the previous mouse is nearby, the beetle goes to it and ignores the substitute. Probably this indicates that a burying beetle somehow adds a distinctive scent to its prize, and returns to this as a mark of ownership.

Some European scientists have tested burying beetles in another way. First, a small daub of red nail enamel is added to the top of the insect's body to make it recognizable as an individual. Then the beetle is carried unharmed in a closed box some distance from the trophy it has been attending. Upon release, the insect has an opportunity to fly back to the small body or to find another and not be seen again. Some of these marked beetles have returned from as much as two and one-half miles away, and resumed work on the same dead body within less than two days' time. Surely this shows a surprisingly long memory, or an incredible sensitivity to the odor of decay, as well as that

Small burying beetle, head downward, on side of dead mouse, sending into the breeze a chemical call for help

a large area offers very few dead bodies as targets for the beetles.

Each beetle to arrive first tests the dead body for size. Quite often the prize is too big for one small beetle, yet is free to move and manageable with help. A small beetle shows that it has another trick ready for this emergency. The insect has no need to abandon a dead squirrel. It may climb, instead, up the side of the body and turn into a vertical position, head downward. A faint fragrance is released for the breeze to carry. This perfume appeals to other burying beetles of the same kind and opposite sex. The distinctive chemical message brings them flying upwind, lured from great distances by the special scent. A dozen or more may arrive at the body. Immediately there is a battle. Clicking and clawing at one another, the beetles struggle. Weaker and smaller ones give up and fly away. One victor is left to assist with the work, and to become the mate of the beetle that signaled for help.

Burying beetles, both male and female, come in a range of sizes within each species. Yet no detail evident to the human eye or nose reveals which sex is which. No doubt the insects themselves tell easily by scent. Each individual tolerates a member of the same species and opposite sex, but not another of the same sex, and often not individuals of smaller, different species. Unwelcome individuals generally leave after a few confrontations. The remaining pair rarely take time for courtship until they have a dead body of suitable size buried securely. Whatever pair work together become mates later on. By then, each one has worked so hard that it has a right to share the buried food, and to participate in rearing a family.

5.

Hitchhiking Helpers

Almost every burying beetle has tiny companions. They are brownish pink spider mites, scarcely $\frac{1}{64}$th inch in length. A dozen or more may run about over the body of a beetle, and cling to the insect wherever it goes. Only if a mite runs out on an antenna is the beetle likely to reach up a foot and kick off the mite. Some of the mites scamper off while a burying beetle investigates a dead mouse or a bird it has found. Usually they hurry back from among the fur or feathers, climbing to ride pickaback on the beetle before it moves away or underneath.

Actually the mites are not as plain colored as they appear to the unaided eye. Through a powerful lens, the eight legs of each mite are seen to be variegated in a pattern of pale and darker spots. This is why the mites have been

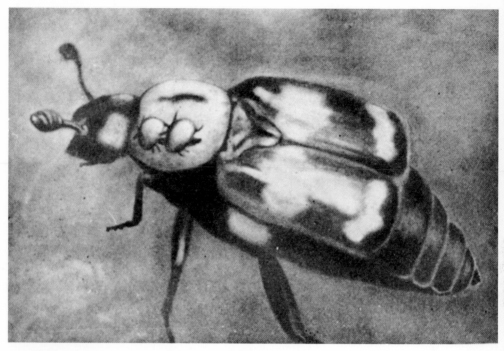
Burying beetle with two mites on top of thorax

given the scientific name *Poecilochirus* (pronounced pee-sea'-low-kigh-russ), from the Greek words for "pied claws," as though their legs at least were dressed like those of the pied piper.

At first the pinkish mites were suspected of being parasites. Perhaps they pushed their needle-sharp mouthparts through the joint membranes of a beetle and sucked its blood. Maybe they took nourishment in this way from beetle larvae without killing them. Then a British scientist learned that the mites may actually help the beetles. The mites suck the contents from eggs laid by flies on the dead body. Then no maggots hatch to compete with the beetle larvae for the meat supply. Always the beetles have meat to spare and share with the tiny mites. These reproduce in and around the burial chamber.

Eventually each new burying beetle completes its pupal transformation, gets to its feet, and prepares to push upward through the soil as an adult. The lively mites gather on its body and stay with the insect. They cling to its back, its sides and undersurface, to its legs, and to one another. More than 400 mites can find a place to cling and be carried by a single beetle. They conceal its body as though it were wearing a fuzzy, squirming coat. They must make it difficult for the beetle to see where it is going. Constantly the mites rearrange themselves, especially when the insect spreads its wings in readiness to fly.

Most of the mites fall off and get lost while a burying beetle flies in search of a trophy or a mate. The twenty to forty mites that manage to hold on are the ones that will help protect the food supply for the beetle, and will reproduce many more mites. If only Jean Henri Fabre had known how helpful the mites are, he would not have complained that burying beetles are "abominably verminous." Instead, he would have praised the ability of the insect to fly about while loaded down with helpful hitchhikers.

Scientists everywhere know burying beetles by a name given them in 1781 by a Danish biologist, who chose *Nicrophorus* (pronounced nick-roff'-or-us) from the

Greek words for "carriers of the dead." A century ago, people knew these insects as "sexton beetles," at a time when the sexton at the church was also the digger of graves in the cemetery. But whether carrying or burying, as the situation requires, these versatile insects are helpful neighbors of which we should be aware. They are nature's clean-up crew.

6.

Nature's Undertakers

We know now how small animals disappear and why. Great numbers of them die every week, yet their bodies rarely stay in sight. Burying beetles tidy up the land so rapidly and efficiently that we overlook them. We should give them full credit for their extraordinary services.

Theirs is a very old way of life. The fossil record shows that burying beetles have been in existence for fully three million years, which is long before the great Ice Age. These insects were working in the same way before the first people—the ancestors of American Indians—came to America. Indians did not reach the Los Angeles region of California until about 12,000 years ago.

Now in Los Angeles, several burying beetles are preserved in the black asphalt of the famous tar pits at La Brea Park. They have been recovered along with the remains of extinct animals, such as ground sloths, saber-toothed tigers, dire wolves, American camels, and native horses and elephants, plus smaller animals, including coyotes almost like those of modern times.

Probably the burying beetles came to attend small animals that got mired in the asphalt beside the big ones about 30,000 years ago. We can think of the insects sliding under the dead bodies and getting their backs stuck in the tar. From then on, they simply sank downward and were preserved, along with the skeletons of the larger animals. All of them made the same mistake by venturing out onto the sticky tar, and paid for it with their lives.

Coyotes still live on the hills around Los Angeles. Their calls often ring out distinctively at night. Some of the same kinds of burying beetles are still there too, carrying on the tradition that goes far back in time. The beetles, like their ancestors, produce new life from larger creatures that perish, and contribute to the fertility of the soil. The need for the beetles in the wild community seems endless. They earn a place on earth more lasting than asphalt or concrete, hills or streams, forests or open country.

Now the future is less bright for some of these amazing insects. The largest of them in America, a kind fully 1½ inches long, are scarce where formerly they were abundant —from Canada to the Gulf states and from the Atlantic coast to the western edge of the Mississippi River basin. They tended larger dead animals, including fishes. Fifty years ago, from Long Island, New York, to New England, these largest burying beetles came by the dozens wherever fishermen disposed of the remains of the fish they caught.

Now this spectacular kind—*Nicrophorus americanus*—is rare.

The most successful collector of the giant burying beetle for museums was Mr. Roy Latham of Orient, New York. In his ninety-sixth year he wrote that he used to trap fish as a business, pack salable fish in ice and ship them to the Fulton Fish Market in New York City. During the 1920s he always had:

> ". . . plenty of fish. I used to put ½ bushel of fish, more or less, in a burlap bag and place it in the back yard among weeds and bushes, leaving the top open. In two, three or more days, dump the bag out. I always expected to see six to eight beetles and once had a record of 22 *americanus* and several of the smaller species. *Americanus* was always the most common [species] of the genus here.
>
> "We were also in the farming business and spread all the unmarketable fish on the land for fertilizer. We used to get fish by the boat full and carted them to the farm by horse and wagon and spread the trash fish from the wagon with pitchforks. On warm nights in summer the air around the farm was savory with the stench of spoiling fish. This evidently was the reason for their abundance in Orient. They [the beetles] were drawn in by the smelly rotting fish odor in the air. After they passed laws to stop spreading fish on the land, the 'stinking bug,' as we called them on the farm, stopped coming and disappeared completely from Orient."

Burying beetles often fly to lighted windows and cling to the screen at night.

The giant burying beetles have vanished from almost everywhere. In fact, the last twenty-four of these insects to be seen at all have flown not to bait of any kind. They have blundered into ultraviolet traplights shining at night to attract other insects from the woods and fields. This is the only method that has succeeded recently, and even it has failed since 1974, as though the giant American burying beetle was extinct. The ones that came to light between 1951 and 1974 were in Arkansas, Michigan, Missouri, Tennessee, and Ontario, Canada.

People have changed the world for burying beetles, without realizing it. We no longer allow dead fish and fish remains to be left exposed. We approve of the speed with which herring gulls clean up the dead fishes along the coast, before burying beetles can do anything. The gulls are much more numerous than they used to be, because they can space out their natural meals with edible garbage from city dumps. New methods of treating wastes may improve this situation, and indirectly help the beetles.

In many parts of the country, garbage that has not yet been collected for sanitary disposal attracts raccoons and skunks. The numbers of these mammals have increased too. Both scavenge in darkness and devour small bodies wherever these may be. In many regions they dispose of such materials, leaving nothing that a beetle can use. If the hard-working beetles arrive first, the skunk may eat them too.

Burying beetles have no way to defend themselves against the scavenging mammals that are abroad at night.

A common burying beetle, only about an inch long.

Nor is anyone except an admirer likely to put up a strong wire fence around a dead mouse or a sparrow, to let the insects through while keeping out the hungry mammals. Fencing can be done if a person is determined to improve opportunities for observation. It is one way to gain a sense of exploring the living earth, starting close to home as though on a research expedition.

Our planet may still have another very large burying beetle, one more than 1½ inches long. Whether it is doing well or poorly continues to be a mystery. It is a native to China, from which reports may again become available with improvements in communication. Perhaps some of these big Chinese insects might fly to an ultraviolet light shining at night in a suitable place. Scientists in the Western world wish someone would find out and spread the news.

It seems appropriate that beetles of some kind should serve as nature's undertakers. Beetles have prospered and become more diverse than insects of any other type, actually more than other forms of animal life. Scientists have discovered a grand total of about 1,005,000 species of animals, of which nearly 700,000 are insects, and around 300,000 are beetles. Each species has its own life-style, its time-tested program for success, its own geographic range. For about 100 of these beetle species, the way has been by burying small dead animals and turning their remains to good use for a better earth.

Index

ABOUT THE AUTHORS

Lorus J. Milne was born in Toronto, Canada, and developed an interest in insects as a boy. As a teenager, he encountered burying beetles near a cottage in the Ontario wilderness. His insect collection won first prize at the Canadian National Exhibition and led later to a position with the Canadian government, financing his education at the University of Toronto. After completing his formal studies as a professional biologist, with a Ph.D. degree from Harvard University, he and his American-born wife Margery (Ph.D., Radcliffe College) returned to the Ontario site for further observations. They made a color movie of beetle activities to show at science meetings, because many biologists doubted that insects could perform so many amazing feats in transporting and burying small animals, and that the male beetle would assist so regularly. These beetle activities can be witnessed over most of America, even within sight of the campus of the University of New Hampshire, where both authors teach.